First published in India by HarperCollins *Children's* Books 2025
An imprint of HarperCollins *Publishers* India
HarperCollins *Publishers* India, Cyber City, Building 10-A, Gurugram,
Haryana-122002, India
www.harpercollins.co.in

2 4 6 8 10 9 7 5 3 1

Text Copyright © Shobha Tharoor Srinivasan 2025
Illustrations Copyright © Isha Nagar 2025

P-ISBN: 978-93-6989-238-9
E-ISBN: 978-93-6989-976-0

The views and opinions expressed in this book are the author's own and the facts are as reported by her. The publishers are not in any way liable for the same.

Shobha Tharoor Srinivasan asserts the moral right to be identified as the author of this work.

All rights reserved. No part of this publication may be reproduced, stored in a retrieval system, or transmitted, in any form or by any means, electronic, mechanical, photocopying, recording or otherwise, without the prior permission of the publishers.

Without limiting the exclusive rights of any author, contributor or the publisher of this publication, any unauthorized use of this publication to train generative artificial intelligence (AI) technologies is expressly prohibited. HarperCollins also exercise their rights under Article 4(3) of the Digital Single Market Directive 2019/790 and expressly reserve this publication from the text and data-mining exception.

Typeset in Crimson text 10.5pt/15 by Isha Nagar
Inside illustrations and cover design by Isha Nagar

Printed and bound at Thomson Press India Ltd

*

HarperCollins Publishers, Macken House, 39/40 Mayor Street Upper, Dublin 1, D01 C9W8, Ireland

This book is produced from independently certified FSC® paper to ensure responsible forest management.

SPEAK SMARTER   WRITE STRONGER

SHOBHA THAROOR SRINIVASAN

Illustrated by
Isha Nagar

HARPERCOLLINS
CHILDREN'S BOOKS

Words are not as satisfactory as we should like them to be. But, like our neighbours, we have got to live with them and must make the best and not the worst of them.

—Samuel Butler

CONTENTS

- Let Me Tell You About the ALPHABET — 11
- Rations and Appellations — 42
- Small and Simple Are Not the Same Thing — 45
- Figurative Speech — 52
- Did You Just Say That? — 62
- What Can You Do with Your Words? — 68
- How Many Sounds Can a C Make? — 72
- The Sound of Silence — 74
- Vocabulary—Zany Words from A to Z — 76
- Parts of Speech — 80
- Epilogue — 83
- On Words — 86

Introduction

Words seem to matter more than ever these days. Whether we speak them in powerful oratories, or write them in long essays, or use them judiciously with the 280 characters allowed on X (previously Twitter), or even when we text hastily on our phones, words are what help us communicate with others. Words can move us to tears or make us laugh aloud. And words used efficiently can inspire us and call us to action.

But, when used in error, words no longer hold their meaning, and the attempted communication is hampered. To quote the celebrated American author Mark Twain, 'The difference between the right word and the almost right word is really a large matter—it is the difference between lightning and a lightning bug.'

We know that errors can be hilarious, as when we mistakenly use a word in place of a similar sounding one with unintentionally amusing effect. These gaffes are known as malapropisms. Though the word comes from the character Mrs Malaprop in Richard Sheridan's play *The Rivals*, who said 'illiterate him from your thoughts' when she meant 'obliterate', many well-known figures in history have also used words incorrectly. The American president George W. Bush was known to make up a word or two. When Bush watched his approval rating plummet, he lamented that he was 'misunderestimated' by people. What he meant to say, of course, was that he was 'misunderstood' and 'underestimated'. Such 'Bushisms' have been collected by wordsmiths over the years and have been published as humour books.

Sometimes the wrong word can create misunderstandings. We have all suffered the indignities of inadvertent gaffes with our smartphones' autocorrect feature. The story of the person who meant to say 'you are dear to me' that was inadvertently transposed to 'you are dead to me' and ended a close friendship comes to mind. One thing that we can all agree on, however, is that words are powerful. When words are organized efficiently, using proper grammatical structures, their meaning helps us communicate effectively.

I have written this book, which is part poetry, part prose, part vocabulary list, part literary text and part story, as a fun way to learn how to use words effectively. As you will see, words are like clay: they can be moulded, changed, expanded and shrunk, to fit the purpose of our communication.

To quote British Author and graphic novelist Neil Gaiman, 'The one thing that you have that nobody else has is you. Your voice, your mind, your story, your vision. So write and draw and build and play and dance and live as only you can!'

> **Words** *are sacred. If you get the right ones in the right order, you can nudge the world a little.*
>
> —Tom Stoppard, British playwright

Let Me Tell You About the ALPHABET

Though the English language is built on just twenty-six letters (for comparison, Hindi has forty-eight, Malayalam has fifty-six and Tamil has a whopping two hundred and forty-seven), its word creation capability is capacious, and English words are capable of conveying multiple meanings. This poem delves into the essence of the English alphabet, exploring its role in shaping language, communication and creativity. It explores the power of each letter, highlighting how these simple symbols form the foundation for an expansive and intricate world of expression. Each letter, with its unique form and sound, serves as a building block for words and ideas, unlocking endless possibilities for expression. In fact, through this exploration, the poem seeks to celebrate the alphabet's significance and invite readers to appreciate its subtle power in everyday life.

The letter **A** is amazing!

It starts the **a**lphabet.

Without it there'd be no **a**stronaut,

And you couldn't be **a**ffectionate.

The letter **A** is **a**wesome!

It's a vowel that begins the list.

Imagine an **a**pple without **A**,

Or spell **A**NT when **A** is missed.

As the first letter of the English alphabet, the letter **A** is associated with beginnings. It is also associated with being the best (**A** grades), being action- or achievement-oriented (type **A**), and for being the first of the five vowels in the alphabet.

Can you think about more **A** words that you know and use regularly? Make a list. What would you like to do with this special letter? How about writing an **a**crostic?

B begins the consonants,
Brings biscuits with our tea.
Breaks down those boastful questions,
Like 'To be or not to be?'
B helps us hear big notes and sounds,
Like the buzzing of a bee.
B tells stories of battles and wars,
Of bullies and BIG bravery.

The Latin alphabet, which forms the basis for many European languages, has **B** as its second letter. It is also the second letter in languages such as English, Spanish, French, German, Italian, Portuguese, Dutch, Swedish, Finnish and others, since they all use the Latin alphabet. Here is a delightful tongue twister that I use in my introductory class on *Voice Over Basics* that is fun to say aloud.

Betty Botter bought a bit of butter.
The butter Betty Botter bought was bitter.
So, Betty Botter bought a bit of better butter,
To make the bitter butter Betty Botter bought better.

Give it a try! How fast can you say it? Do you know any other tongue twisters?

C cuddles us in its loopy form,

Comes close with its curvaceous letter.

C offers comfort and camaraderie,

And care, so chums can feel better.

C helps us carve, C helps us catch,

Calls us to cricket, and to chess.

C helps us cut, C crafts our style,

Contains colours, and clears the mess.

C is the third letter in the modern English alphabet. It is often pronounced like the sound /s/, but depending on the letters that follow the letter c in a word, it can sound hard like the /k/ sound. Read the poem called 'How Many Sounds Can a C Make?', which I have included in this book. Can you think of other letters in the English alphabet that sound different depending on their position in a word? Look for the poem called the 'Sound of Silence' to know more.

D

Different **D** you'll soon **d**iscover,
Drums and **d**ances with **d**isco flair.
Developing **d**rama is a **d**istinct feat,
Drowned in **d**oldrums and **d**espair!
D is **d**oubtful, **d**eviant and **d**istant,
Difficult, and **d**isdainful too.
Don't **d**ismiss it quite so fast,
Delightful as well it **d**oes **d**o.

D is for drama. Can you think of a dramatic game to play in which you perform the words rather than say them out aloud? There's a game called 'Charades' which does just that and when you play it you will realize how challenging (and hilarious) it is to communicate without speaking your words.

E is for **e**lephant, **e**agle and **e**land,

Ermine, **e**gret, **e**els as well.

Entrance to **E**nglish, most **e**loquent language,

Enthused **e**ducators **e**mbrace and tell.

Emphatic this letter, **e**mbellishes forever,

Effortless, **e**xceptional, **e**very word.

Epic thoughts **e**voked, **e**ach idea proposed,

Echoes **e**xcitement, and **e**xclaims to be heard!

E is the second vowel and most used letter of the English alphabet. Here is a fun word game to play: come up with 20 five-letter (or longer) words that **do not** use the letter E.

Flighty F with forked fingers can fret,

For fierce foes can be a formidable force.

Though fearful sometimes, F forgives and is friend,

Fantastic, a fun-loving source!

Freckled face, five long fingers and forehead,

Fast feet, full-fledged and fab-four.

F frames these words, fixes and fashions,

And feathers and forges five more.

Can you write more words with the letter **F**? What is the longest word starting with **F** that you know? **F** is for family. What word games do you play with your family? I enjoyed both Scrabble and Boggle when I was growing up.

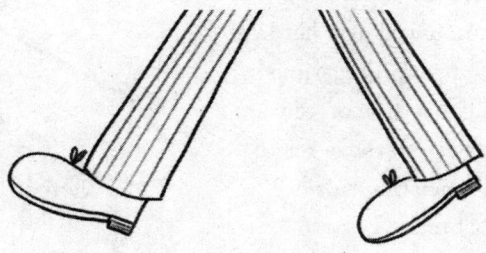

G

G gives us **G**od, **g**ift and **g**ather,

Garrulous, **g**enerous and **g**aze.

Gentlemen, **g**irls, and **g**o-**g**etters,

Gorillas, and **g**iraffes that **g**raze.

G grows **g**reen **g**rass, **g**rapes and **g**arlic,

Gallops and **g**oes **g**aily to **g**ames.

Giggles, **g**rins and **g**ushes,

Groans, **g**rowls, **g**athers and **g**ains.

G is one of those rule-breaking letters. G followed by the vowels e, i or y is usually pronounced as the /dʒ/ sound, as in angel, agile or gypsy. But there's the Indian name 'Ragini' which is a rule breaker, where the letter is pronounced as /g/. 'Anger' is another rule breaker. Some words where the letter is pronounced as a hard /g/ sound include 'anger', 'gregarious' or 'wrong'. Make a list of ten words with G and see if the letter follows the pronunciation rule or is more of a rule breaker!

H is **h**eavy and **h**ungry and **h**asty,
Humble, and **h**umorous too.
Hefty **h**aul it can **h**eave like **h**eifers,
And **h**ysterical, **h**ilarious do.
H has **h**im, and **h**er, and **h**uman,
Hale and **h**earty, **h**ugs and **h**aze.
House, **h**ome, **h**earth is **h**arnessed,
H **h**olds **h**ostages in place.

The letter **H** is often silent in English when it follows the letter c, like in character and charisma, or at the beginning of words that are borrowed from French, such as hour or honest. Also, speakers in different parts of the world have their own idiosyncrasies—for example you can hear the sound /h/ in the word 'herb' if a British person is speaking, but many Americans pronounce it like 'erb.'

'**H**ad to Declare' is a fun word game where you name an object and imagine the city/place where you could have bought it, such that the name of the object and the city/place are in rhyme. So, you could say 'I bought a tunic in Munich' or 'I bought corn in Bonn' or 'I bought some jelly in New Delhi!' This game teaches you about places all over the world and helps you practice your rhyming skills as well.

I intersects between the vowels,

Is an individual, impressive letter.

Inspires imagination, and instruction,

Includes idioms that inform us better.

Innocent, inscrutable, infectious,

I identifies in an inimitable manner.

If imperial is your image, or informal,

I injects style and improves the planner.

I is the third vowel in the English alphabet. I is not used as often in words as 'E', but you will discover, when you are playing a word game like Scrabble, how hard it is to make a high-scoring word without the right vowel. When my children were little, we played 'One word makes little, little words' at home. How many three- or four-letter words can you make from the letters in the word 'imagination'? This is an interesting and challenging exercise. Set a timer and give it a try with your friend or sibling.

Jovial, jocular, jokester,
J jiggles and jogs on the path.
Jumps, joyfully jives through the letters,
Juvenile in jousts in the bath.
Jaguars and jackals in the jungle,
Jingling jewellery just like a bell.
Jam, jelly and juice, J can bottle,
Jackfruit and jaggery as well.

J is for journal. Have you ever tried to keep a journal or a dream diary? This sort of record-keeping is such an interesting and entertaining way to process your thoughts and feelings. It's also a way of keeping a daily record of occurrences, experiences or observations when you are traveling. I did, and that is why I was able to share my travel sestudes in this book. You too could try writing a journal entry!

Kingly **K** of **K**ashmir and **K**iev,
Kabul, **K**ansas and **K**uala Lumpur.
Kwanza, **k**ibbutz and **k**ismet,
Knowledge of **k**leptocracy and more.
Krait, **k**ite and **k**ingfisher,
Killer whale, **k**eeshond, **k**angaroo.
K starts **k**nife, **k**itten and **k**illjoy,
Kinship, **k**iss and **k**indness too.

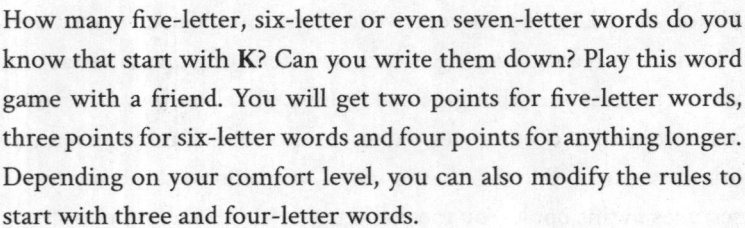

How many five-letter, six-letter or even seven-letter words do you know that start with **K**? Can you write them down? Play this word game with a friend. You will get two points for five-letter words, three points for six-letter words and four points for anything longer. Depending on your comfort level, you can also modify the rules to start with three and four-letter words.

Lean, limber and lissome a letter,

L lights up life, brings lamps their lustre.

La lingers in song, lilts to music,

Listens to loud laughter and bluster.

Left-handed, listless, lethargic,

Lonesome say the lads seeking mates;

But L's lighthearted, loving, languorous,

Loquacious, and limitless, when late.

When I see the letter L, laugh comes to mind. Recently, I did a fun writing exercise with my granddaughter that was reminiscent of Mad Libs, the word game where one player prompts another for a list of words to fill up the blanks in a pre-made story. The result is a laugh-out-loud crazy tale. When Mrinalini and I played, we wrote a story using only a dozen words that I had solicited from her, using prompts like 'name a noun,' 'a verb', 'a part of the body' and 'an animal', and then we had to build a story from the words suggested. There were many laughs while we wrote, and we had the most hilarious tale to recount to the rest of the family when we were done.

Want to give it a try?

Most meaningful M is mother,
Moment, musical, and man.
Magic adds marvel to mystery,
M means magnificent just began.
Mighty, masterly, marvellous,
Manipulating modesty, and more.
M meanders and moves with a mission,
Making macaw and minotaur.

Malayalam is a word starting with the letter **M**. It is also a palindrome—a word that reads the same backward or forward. Madam is another palindrome. Can you think of any other palindromes? They can start with any letter of the alphabet. They can also be phrases. Make a list of such words/phrases to share.

N

Naughty or **N**ice? is the question;
N **n**ormally **n**otes with a **n**ame.
Not always **n**ew, but **n**atural,
Nosy, kind **n**eighbour all the same.
Naïve, **n**arcissistic and **n**oisy,
Nervous of **n**ightmares at **n**ight.
N **n**otes words in the **n**ewspaper,
Neanderthals, **n**eurons enlight.

'No Words' or 'Secret Words' is another fun game. One person thinks up a word and has to explain it to their partner using images. So, if you are thinking of the word SOFT, you will need to draw four objects, each representing words that start with S, O, F and T. You could draw a sun, an orange, a frame and a table. So, there are no letters (only images) in your clues but the answer is a word.

Oranges, orchids and omelettes,

In the **o**ffice are **o**ften **o**n **o**ffer.

But the **o**wl, **o**strich and **o**rangutan,

Are in an ark **o**r a zoo's c**o**ffer.

Oh without **O** will be wordless,

Omnipresent vowel, **o**rdained and bold.

Obnoxious, **o**afish, **o**bese,

Yet **o**bliging, **o**bedient and **o**ld.

O is for **O**ne and here's an **o**riginal idea—**o**ne-word stories. Each player in a circle says **o**ne word and the next player adds another word to advance the story. If this game is too easy, you can make it more challenging by only adding words that rhyme.

Proud, prancing **P** is a **p**ennant,
Or **p**owerful **p**rose on **p**aper for a **p**al.
P **p**okes and **p**ricks and is **p**ompous,
Playful and **p**ure-hearted a gal.
Predilection, **p**unishment, **p**oetry,
Plates of **p**izza and **p**ie to be **p**aid.
Also **p**ituitary and **p**ineal in our body,
Purposefully **p**repared and made.

You must have all read **p**icture books when you were young. These short books expand a child's imagination by introducing them to new characters, settings, dilemmas and sources of laughter through pictures and colours. As children, my siblings and I played a game where we 'painted verbal pictures' with our words for descriptions. My brother usually started the story, and the rule was that it had to be vivid and dramatic tale. He would stop after two sentences, and the next **p**layer had to use words to 'colour' the tale further. We came up with some bizarre but brilliant and often very funny stories. Do try to **p**aint a story with your friends and family!

Q without u makes **Q**at,

Qwerty (keyboard) not **q**uite as well.

Words like **q**uarrel, **q**uibble, **q**uiz,

And **q**uick, in Scrabble games can spell.

Quilt, **q**ueen, **q**uad, and **q**uestion,

Quagmire, **q**ueue, **q**uinoa and **q**uill.

When in a **q**uandary or on a **q**uay,

There are **q**uintuple ways to chill.

One school of thought for the shape of the letter **Q** is that the way we write it has its origin in Egyptian hieroglyphics—the hieroglyph for a cord of wool, which was pronounced as 'qaw', looks similar to the letter. There are **q**uintuple ways to entertain yourself (love the musicality of this **Q** word, which means five). There's a board game called Qwirkle that I play at home. Players score points by creating lines of tiles that are either all the same colour or all the same shape, aiming for a 'Qwirkle' (a line of six tiles). The player with the most points at the end wins.

Royal R makes the word Regal,
Robust, rich and rarely rude.
R also makes rascally rogues ready,
And restless rakes, reasonably lewd.
Radical, responsible and reasoned,
Radiant, rambunctious, red as well.
R remembers the reason for reckon,
Remain, runway, and rouse it tells

'Read' is my favourite R word. If you read you know that you are learning new words every day. Soon you will be able to play 'Human Thesaurus'. Here's how you play the game. Choose a simple word like 'clever'. Think of as many synonyms for this word as you can. If playing with others, you can set a timer and trade off with different words, or write words down and see who can come up with the most.

Sibilant **S** can be silly,

Sometimes **s**oft, but **s**trident too.

Sensitive, **s**ensible, yet **s**o very **s**assy,

Strong willed, **s**harp tongued, a crotchety **s**hrew.

Scones, **s**hrimp and **s**almon start with **S**,

Sausage or **s**teak, and **s**tew as well.

Sautéed or **s**tirred, **s**hredded or **s**harpened,

Salty **s**nacks and **s**avouries **s**ell.

Spoken-word poetry starts with **S**. Do you know what the term refers to? This S-word refers to an oral poetic performance, one in which the poem is not just read aloud but performed, with rhyme, repetition, improvisation and word play. In fact, spoken word poems frequently address issues of social justice, politics, race and other important subjects that prompt deep feeling and expression from the performer. You can experiment with spoken-word poetry by creating your own 'at-home' theatre to practice.

T

Transformative **T** teases in **t**ime,

Takes the **t**rouble to **t**alk in **t**une.

T **t**aps a sound, that informs the words,

Taking **t**ourists from **t**rees to dune!

Tiramisu or **t**reacle,

T **t**itillates the **t**ongue.

Telling **t**ales, **T** **t**ravels far,

Triumphant **TTT** is rung!

There's a wonderful vocabulary game called 'Table' that you can play in teams. Perhaps you know it? First set up two teams with at least two players on each team. Draw a table on a page or whiteboard with categories like colour, animal, name, sport, food, etc. as the headings. Pick a letter at random from a bag of letters. Suppose you pick **T**. You need to come up with T-words in all these categories (for example, turquoise, tiger, Tara, tennis, tortilla). The team that finishes first can call out 'Stop the Bus'! and win the maximum points for that round. Repeat the rounds. Fun, isn't it? I've heard a lot of laughs when children play this game.

U is not you but starts **u**mbrella,

Unicorn, **U**ruguay and **u**rn.

Use U for space in consonants,

Understand U as vowel, we learn.

Umm, **u**ff, **u**gh is **u**lulated,

Urchins and **u**ncles are called.

Under or **u**nable or **u**gly,

Without U **u**nderwriting is stalled!

Our family's favourite board game is Scrabble. But sometimes, when we have completed the game, we play something called 'Unscrabble'. Unscrabble is not just an interesting U-word. It is when you get to count the points on the number of tiles you take away from the Scrabble board while leaving complete words behind. This game can help hone vocabulary and spelling skills and is a great way to spend time if you are stuck indoors on a rainy day. Try Unscrabble today!

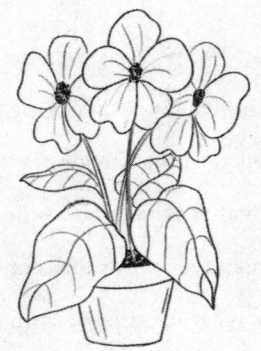

Viva **V**, **v**ictorious and **v**ibrant,
Vital, **v**aliant, and **v**ogue.
Visit this **v**aluable letter,
Very **v**ersatile, a clever rogue!
Valid **v**eteran **v**iews with a purpose,
Vigorous **V** gives rhythm to **v**erse.
Violets in a **v**ase and warm **v**egetables,
Viper's sting sends us **v**enting to the nurse.

I was looking up animals that start with the letter **V** in English and discovered that there are not very many. Of course, most of us know vulture, viper and perhaps the carnivorous plant, the Venus flytrap. Here are some other animals that start with **V** that I found—vampire bat, vampire squid, vermilion flycatcher (a small bird), vervet monkey, vine snake (long-nosed whip snake), viper shark (viper dogfish), Vizsla (dog breed) and volcano snail. You can look up other **V** words in a different category. Perhaps plants since I've started that for you?

W

What? Why? Well, says the letter **W**,

Wisdom and **w**it, **w**orking powers.

When **w**ishing for some **w**onder,

We **w**atch **w**hales and **w**ildflowers.

Women are **w**ordsmiths of **W**,

They **w**ear it **w**ith **w**armth and **w**ow.

Warm-hearted **w**ell-**w**ishers are **w**orthy,

Watchful, letter **W** takes a bow!

W is for **word** search. You could create a word puzzle and a list of words to find in it. Then challenge a friend or sibling to find all the words in a set number of minutes. Perhaps a dozen words in five minutes? This is a challenge both for the word search creator and the one who finds the words. This word puzzle will soon become your favourite game.

Xerox, Xenia and Xeric,
Of machines, plants and moisture do say.
X words like xylophones tinkle,
Travel abroad? Xenophiles may!
X marks eXit, X-Ray and Xmas,
Xavier and Xebec too.
X sounds like other letters,
But X in Math is mostly a clue.

Thinking of words that include **X** is quite a challenge. I realized this when I wrote this poem. How many words do you know that use the letter **X**? Write down a list of **X**-words. It does not matter whether **X** starts the word or is in it. But do make sure that you know the meaning of each word you list.

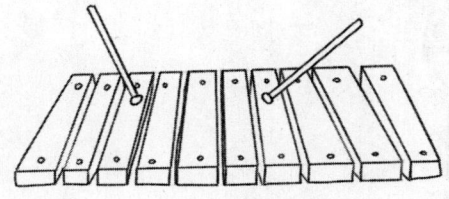

Yoghurt, and **y**eti, and **y**ardstick,
Are musical **Y**-words you speak.
Yule logs, and egg **y**olks, and **y**east,
Despite the holiday **y**ams can reek!
The **y**outhful stay **y**oung with **y**oga,
They hike **Y**osemite and the **Y**ucatan.
Yesterday's **y**okels were **y**apping,
YouTube's **y**ells changed the nature of man.

Y starts the word *You*. Dear reader, you are the most important ingredient in this book. It is what you bring to these pages and what you take away that makes this unique book work. I hope that you have enjoyed the games that accompany this alphabet poem and that you will play some of them with your friends.

☆ Z ☆

Zealous Zayn was zestful in Zambia,
Zaccharaia had a zeal to be zen.
Zenobia zeroed on zealotry,
Zara zig-zagged on paper with pen.
Zebu or Zebra in Zaire,
Zeitgeist of this period so bold.
Z is the zenith letter,
With EEs or ED Z is told.

When my children were learning the alphabet in school in America, they used to sing *The Alphabet Song*, which went A, B, C, D, E, F, G and Z rhymed with G. You can listen to the song here: https://www.youtube.com/watch?v=75p-N9YKqNo&ab_channel=KidsTV123 Of course, I grew up pronouncing the letter as zed, which would not have worked for this song. We think of Z as the last letter of the English alphabet, but I learned in a *Readers Digest* article that Z was actually not the last to be included in the alphabet. Evidently 'J' joined the alphabet later. There were also six more letters in the English alphabet that were dropped many years ago. Interesting what you can learn when you take the time to read!

SCORECARD

PLAYER NAME	Aryaa		
WORD GAME			
WORD PUZZLE	12TH APRIL	45/50 (1st Rank)	
UNSCRABBLE	18TH APRIL	26/50 (3rd Rank)	
QWIRKLE	22ND APRIL	34/50 (2nd Rank)	
SECRET WORDS	29TH APRIL	48/50 (2nd Rank)	
TABLE	10TH MAY	38/50 (2nd Rank)	

Now that you have learned about the alphabet, think about the first letter of your name, and list a few words starting with that letter that describe you best. Write a paragraph about yourself, and try to include words beginning with as many letters of the alphabet as possible.

Rations and Appellations

When the right name is the wrong one, words (and names) do matter.

Muthashan, my grandfather, pandered to our growing curiosity in such an expressive manner. His box of stories, like Pandora's, was constantly full, and an engaged and appreciative audience was always welcome where he lounged, newspaper in hand, on his easy chair.

Yet, Muthashan had a weakness. Like many storytellers, he loved telling his favourite story—about how he got his name—and that's the story we heard most often.

'Children, you all know about the time I went to England.' We smiled, remembering the many tales about Muthashan and his two brothers, just out of a village preparatory school, gawky and shy in an alien land.

'Well, this was immediately on our arrival, when the post war years had lent a cold and forlorn temperament to what we later discovered was an otherwise vibrant city. My older brother, who had brought us all to England and was responsible for our living arrangements, said that it was essential we get ration cards issued to our names immediately. Since I was the eldest of the three that he brought to the country, I was the obvious person to be in charge of this group. With an air of bravado that I was far from feeling, I marched my brothers up to the ration shop at the end of the road.' We began to nod in mirth as we listened, laughter escaping us as we remembered Muthashan's impending doom.

He continued after the grave pause: 'A lengthy queue awaited us. I hitched up my trousers (quite foreign to my body), beckoned to my brothers and stepped into line. A considerable wait saw us in front of the proverbial English rose—blue eyes and blonde hair swam in front of my eyes, and I hiccupped nervously. She smiled in understanding and waited. The silence grew unbearable and, aware of a mile of men behind me, I decided to get on with it. My fingers motioned three, my mouth formed the word "ration". "Are you all brothers then?" she asked. I nodded vigorously. "Well, you only need one form. Go over to that table and fill it." I nodded again in assent and, with a final tug on the trousers, ambled over to the indicated table. In my best handwriting I filled the form, neatly ascribing our three names with the initial of the family in front. This was the way we did it in Kerala, a surname as unknown to us as a tree-top to a dog.

'Soon we faced her again, this time a little more confident. She ran an expert eye over the page and exclaimed, "I thought you were brothers?" "Yes," I said cheerfully. She beamed as if with some great realization. "Oh, you have different fathers!"

'Unable to protest with the necessary admonishment, I stuttered, and then gasped. "Ayyo, nahi, no, no." She smiled again, quite unperturbed. "Then these are your Christian names!" More than upset at this blasphemy, I cried, "We are Hindus!" "What is that?" she said. Our ten gods laughed silently.

'A protracted verbal battle followed, during which our English rose bloomed with brilliance, and, noticing the common initial before our names, inquired of it eagerly. "That is our family name," said I, not quite modestly. "Well then, since the three of you belong to the same family," —there was a sly smile directed at me just then—"that must be your surname, young man."'

Having reached the end of his story, Muthashan cleared his throat and said, 'So children, that was how we got our name.' His eyes twinkled, and his lips parted in a grin, revealing paan-stained teeth.

Within minutes he was back in that fair land he once knew where an English rose fluttered free in the breeze, beckoning to him.

The most valuable of all talents is that of never using two words when one will do.

—Thomas Jefferson, former president of the United States

Small and Simple Are Not the Same Thing

100-word stories make the writer question each word. The exercise of composing brief narratives with precision is a challenging yet fun exercise that shows the reader how very effective the right words can be. A short story writer needs to be very careful about their choice of words to convey ideas in as succinct a way as possible. Read these 100-word stories and write some of your own. I have included some stories with a few blanks for you to fill, just to get you started.

⭐ THE ISLAND FAR AWAY ⭐

The island far away is not an island. It is a house framed by palm trees and paddy fields and the benevolent peaks of the Western Ghats in southern India. The structure stands tall in the midst of it all, like a piece of land surrounded by shimmering sea. We call it 'Mundarath'—the grand place where the family gathers. Tiled roof, strong teak pillars holding walls together, mango and jackfruit trees offering shade and a deep well to quench our thirst. My grandmother reigns lovingly here. She brings us home, tells us stories and reminds us of our past.

⭐ THE TRAIN STATION ⭐

We were told that the Kerala Express would stop at Palakkad Junction for at least ten minutes. Ours was a large family group and we had at least a dozen suitcases between us. The train rolled in. The younger, sturdier folks started hoisting the luggage into the compartment as the rest of us boarded. A loud whistle broke our momentum. The train had barely been a minute at the station, but we could feel the lurch as it began to pick up speed. I watched in horror as the locomotive pulled away and my two suitcases remained on the platform.

⭐ A KIDNAPPED TEDDY BEAR ⭐

The washerwoman came with her daughter to pick up our clothes. I sat on the porch step with my teddy bear as my mother counted the sheets and saris to be washed. She had just been handed the stack of crisp, clean, laundered clothes from last week. I wanted to show my bear how laundry is done. But something happened in the confusion of the counting and collecting, and my teddy disappeared. I cried and cried. It wasn't until the washerwoman came back on Friday with my bear that we learned that he had been kidnapped along with the clothes!

☆ AN UNEXPECTED ADVENTURE ☆

I left the sheltered life of a village in Kerala for the big city of Calcutta after my wedding. It was a time of excitement, the newness of a man and a marriage, but I did not know what more was in store. Within a week of my arrival in the city, my husband announced that his former boss had offered him a better job in London. We swiftly applied for my passport, converted one first class ticket to two economy passages on the next ship that was sailing and used the extra money for winter clothes. An adventure awaited!

☆ A TOWN MADE OF FOOD ☆

We went to the Carnival World Buffet in Las Vegas. It's considered to be one of the 'must do' activities in Sin City. Right up there with losing your dollars in the casinos, singing to old tunes in the glittering theatres and people watching on the Las Vegas Strip. The buffet was like being in a town made of food. The room was a cavernous space with food stations stretching from one end to the other. You could drown yourself in world cuisine—feasting on food from Asia, from Europe, from the Americas—and savour different flavours till you drop.

☆ A MAD SCIENTIST'S LABORATORY! ☆

Last week, I decided to host a dinner party, and invited ten friends to my home for an Indian meal. They responded to the invitation with the following requests. One couldn't eat onion or garlic. One was vegan and would not eat any dairy. One claimed that lentils gave him gas! Two were vegetarian but did not like green vegetables. One friend ate no pork, the other no fish and three said they preferred a low-carb meal. My well-laid plans to cook a delicious feast turned out, instead, to be the crazed culinary efforts of a mad scientist's laboratory experiment!

In the hope that you will soon write one yourself, I'm going to share a few 100-word stories that you can complete by filling in the blanks. This is like a version of Mad Libs.

A DRAGON EGG

Hatching a dragon egg shouldn't be difficult. But I'm a duck, not a dragon. That's the problem. The story began when my Scottie made friends with Priscilla the dragon. She was the ....

....

....

....

....

....

Today the troublemakers showed up with a huge egg in a wagon. 'You've got to hatch it now or it will never hatch!' they shouted. The egg was dumped out and I was pushed toward the prize. It's been six hours. ....

....

....

....

....

So much for hatching a dragon egg!

AN OBJECT THAT GIVES THE USER SUPERPOWERS

Hey, I found it! I found the glittering rock that's shaped like a butterfly that will give me the powers to fly. It was buried under the moss. I stubbed my toe on the hard surface when I slipped and then noticed the radiating shine. ....
....
....
....
....
....
....
....
....
....

Come on EarthGirl, your WonderWoman is ready to take on the world!

HALLOWEEN

As we thought of creative ways to mask ourselves and maintain a distance from each other during the Covid crisis, I remembered the fun of buying masks ....

....

....

....

....

.... We embraced the joy of carving pumpkins, arranging cobwebs in the front yard, baking treats to share at school and planning and shopping for a new costume for the evening.

....

....

....

....

....

....

DOCTOR'S WAITING ROOM

People sat on bolted-down chairs, awaiting their turn. The fidgety toddler, ...

....

....

.... The young woman, ...

....

The couple, ...

....

.... The woman, ...

....

....

.... The waiting room buzzed with the hum of muted voices and the shuffle of restless feet. Each person here carried ....

....

....

..................................The nurse called out a name. It was someone's turn to move toward the swinging door into a different world— ....

....

....

*To me, the greatest pleasure of writing is not what it is about, but the inner music that **words** make.*

—Truman Capote, American novelist and playwright

Figurative Speech

There are many figures of speech in the English Language. One of my favourites is Onomatopoeia, when a word is formed from the sound associated with it, or the sound that it describes. 'Buzz', 'psst' and 'hiss' are examples. There are other examples of figures of speech that intentionally deviate from the literal language to produce a rhetorical effect. Figurative speech is colourful and expressive. Here are a few poems on terms that are figures of speech.

SPOONERISM

Spoonerism (noun)

Definition: a transposition (usually) of the initial sounds of two or more words (as in *tons of soil* for *sons of toil*). Also, a deliberate verbal error in which a speaker mistakenly transposes the initial sounds or letters of two or more words, often to humorous effect, as in the sentence *you have hissed the mystery lectures*, instead of the intended sentence *you have missed the history lectures*.

Spoonerism

There once was a man who switched words in a phrase,

The results were funny and strange.

His name was William Archibald Spooner,

He taught at Oxford, and ministered on a grange.

So, if you *flutterby*, instead of *butterfly*,

Or there's no *hope in your soul*, there's *soap in your hole*.

Then you've made a speech error that's a 'spoonerism',

And mixing up words is your everyday role!

So, *mean as custard* when it's *keen as mustard*,

Trim your snow tail when *toenails* need trimming.

Birthington's Washday when it's *Washington's birthday*,

Pleating and humming for *Heating and Plumbing*!

When you say *bad salad* for those long *sad ballads*,

When you *plaster man* as you set a *master plan*.

Your brain is running faster than your mouth,

And of spoonerism you are a fan!

OXYMORON

Oxymoron (noun)

Definition: a combination of contradictory words (such as *cruel kindness*); broadly something that is made up of contradictory or incongruous elements

So, who are you calling an oxymoron?

Are you saying you think I am silly?

Did you know that I am a linguistic tool,

Used with thought, not willy-nilly!

I'm a figure of speech, self-contradictory word,

Opposing terms that are used in conjunction.

Think *jumbo shrimp, alone together,*

Small crowd and *farewell reception.*

Yes, oxymoron for rhetorical effect,

Is crafted and created with care.

It can be single word, or adjective and noun,

Or brightened with an adverb–verb pair!

If you're *clearly confused, growing smaller* with worry,

And *weirdly normal* is your *only choice.*

Enjoy this *bittersweet* play of words,

Open secret: oxymorons are not loud noise.

So, who are you calling an oxymoron?

Do you still think that I am silly?

I'm a linguistic tool, a figure of speech,

Used for humour, not willy-nilly!

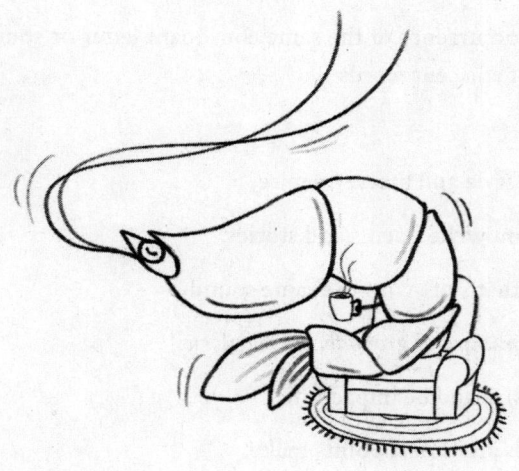

*Sweet words are like honey, a little may refresh,
but too much gluts the stomach.*

—Anne Bradstreet, American poet

ALLITERATION

Alliteration (noun)

Definition: the occurrence of the same consonant letter or sound at the beginning of adjacent words

Alliteration is a style and literary device,

That can help you write poems and stories.

Use two words that start with the same sound,

Like *marvellous music* and *groundbreaking glories*!

You can emphasize and be impactful,

Can stress words and smart points make.

With alliteration your poems will stand out,

Burn bright, sweet and simple, triumphant takes!

Holding hands, humming hymns, singing songs,

Whispering wind, tall trees, mornings misty.

Repeat consonant sounds with a flourish,

Tongue twisters use them, so nifty!

She sells sea-shells on the seashore,

Betty Botter brings butter to bed.

Peter Piper picked peppers for pickles,

Hear the same sound as it is said.

So, use this device when you write,

But remember to exercise limit.

All literary styles have their use,

But too much does not have merit.

*Any **word** you have to hunt for in a thesaurus is the wrong word. There are no exceptions to this rule.*

—Stephen King, American author of supernatural fiction

HYPERBOLE

Hyperbole (noun)

Definition: the use of exaggerated statements or claims that should not be taken seriously or literally

Hyperbole is a tuneful expression,
Four syllables that ring out so clear.
It creates strong impressions and feelings,
As a figure of speech, it is dear.
But hyperbole is exaggeration,
Do not take it so literally.
You are not *hungry enough to eat a horse*,
And it *cost an arm and a leg* is used figuratively.
I know you don't mean it when you say,
That you *walked a million miles* to meet me.
Or that you've seen *Sholay one hundred times*,
You did not *die of embarrassment*, I can see!
He's not *skinny as a toothpick* or *tall as a bean pole*,
She can't *hear a pin drop a mile away*!
But hyperbole is effective,
And used in writing, it does hold sway!

*A **word** is dead when it is said, some say.*
I say it just begins to live that day.

—Emily Dickinson, American poet

PLEONASM

Pleonasm (noun)

Definition: The use of more words than necessary to express an idea, creating a linguistic redundancy

What is this strange word I wondered,

That has almost a plea and a spasm?

It means excessive and is a redundant expression,

Using two words in tandem—*split chasm*.

So *burning fire* and *black darkness*,

I, myself and kick with my feet,

Are examples of words that add little to meaning,

Saw it with my own eyes is hardly a feat!

Pleonasms are used sometimes in error,

Pleonasms are used often in jest.

When emphasis is what you're after,

True fact and *free gift* pass the test.

When you say *I do care*, 'do' is extra,

Why *meet up* when you just need to meet?

But we all use this tool to be emphatic,

And pleonasms we write and repeat!

HETERONYM

Heteronym (noun)

Definition: each of two or more words that are spelled the same but have different pronunciations and meanings

Sometimes words can trip you up,

They look and spell to match.

But though we think they sound the same,

Their difference is the catch!

These heteronyms can twist your tongue,

Like *wound* and *wound* so clear.

His *wound* he cleaned and bandage *wound*,

The difference, did you hear?

Now *dove*, the bird, you know to say,

But when into the pool she *dove*,

Both words spelled same, but listen well,

The second sounds like *cove*.

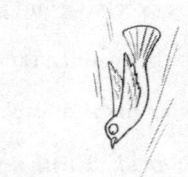

Now *minute* and *minute* on the page,

Use the same letters as you can see.

But the *minute* hole on your dress pants,

Is different from the *minute* until tea.

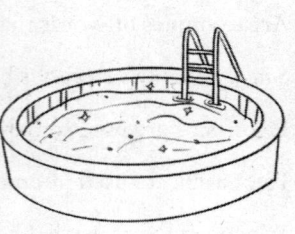

Camels roam the *desert* wide,

On sand they stroll and rest.

But if you *desert* your waiting friend,

You abandon a loving guest.

Now *close* and *close* are still less clear,

They sound so much like each other.

But listen to the sound of 's',

When you *close* the door for mother.

These words are homographs, you see,

And there are others in this row.

Two words spelled alike but not always same,

They can trip us as we go!

__Words__ are like eggs dropped from great heights; you can no more call them back than ignore the mess they leave when they fall.

—Jodi Picoult, American writer

Did You Just Say That?

The English language is always growing and changing. 'Googling' is now an accepted verb for looking things up on the internet, and 'Ayyo' or 'Aiyyo' (a south Indian expression used primarily to express regret, dismay or grief) is now an accepted word in the Oxford English Dictionary. English changes all the time to accommodate its many new speakers. But sometimes that growth is not of a new word added to the language but a phrase incorrectly heard and, because it was bungled in transit, said incorrectly for a long, long time. Sometimes speakers translate directly from another language and the phrase they come up with is not something heard anywhere else in the English-speaking world.

Here are a few commonly misused/misspelled turns of phrase, and examples of Indianisms—some English phrases used only in India.

⭐ ET CETERA BECOMES EXCETERA ⭐

This is a word that is pronounced incorrectly and sometimes spelled incorrectly too. Part of the reason is that it is usually abbreviated as 'etc'. But it is pronounced '*et-ceh-terrah*'. There is no 'x' to be found anywhere and yet I know we continue to spell it with an x.

⭐ FOR ALL 'INTENTS AND PURPOSES'—NOT FOR ALL 'INTENSIVE PURPOSES' ⭐

If you say 'for all intensive purposes', you mean 'for all these very thorough purposes', which doesn't make any sense when you meant to say 'essentially' or 'in effect'.

⭐ UNDOUBTEDLY BECOMES UNDOUBTABLY ⭐

If what you mean is 'without a shadow a doubt', then what you have are two choices, and neither of them is 'undoubtably'. You can either say 'undoubtedly' *or* 'indubitably'. Just don't mash them together and say the wrong thing!

⭐ IS IT REALLY IRONIC? ⭐

Irony involves a reversal. A traffic policeman who has unpaid parking tickets may be in an ironic situation as one would not expect him to neglect the rules that they're supposed to help uphold. But rain on their wedding day is not ironic. It's just wet! And a short man named Shorty is not an example of irony but just a coincidence. But if Shorty was 6 feet tall, that would be ironic!

⭐ ELICIT AND ILLICIT ⭐

When you are trying to get a friend to answer your question, you are trying to elicit a response. Elicit means to coax out or draw forth. But illicit is a whole other story. If you travel on the bus without a ticket, that could be seen as an illicit or improper activity. It contains the word 'ill' in it, which might help you remember and decide which word to use the next time.

⭐ PERQUISITE VERSUS PREREQUISITE ⭐

A 'perquisite', or perk for short, is an extra allowance or privilege. One of the perquisites of my father's old job was a travel allowance for him and his family to visit his hometown once a year. A 'prerequisite' is something that is required before one can continue with a task. So, a prerequisite to applying for college is that you have completed high school.

⭐ ASSENT VERSUS ASCENT ⭐

These two words sound the same so this is an error that usually occurs in writing, where the spelling of the word is important. 'Assent' is when you agree to something, and 'ascent' is a noun that refers to a climb. Edmund Hilary was part of the team that made the first ascent of Mt Everest. Sonali, on the other hand, did not assent to Ravi's marriage proposal.

⭐ FURTHER VERSUS FARTHER ⭐

These are two words that are most often incorrectly used. It is true that both refer to distance, but 'farther' is specific and tangible. You walk thirty feet farther before you turn right to reach the store.

'Further' is meant for figurative distance, when you are not being specific. You have to go a little further to get there. There are exceptions to this rule, but at least for a start remember the tangible and the intangible distance clue.

☆ PASSING OUT ☆

In New York where I went to college, or in California where my daughter did, we would say we 'graduated' when we completed a program of study and left the academic institution. But in India where my cousins studied, they 'passed out' of college. If you pass out in the US, Australia or the UK, you would probably be rushed to a hospital, not congratulated for completing a course of study.

☆ WHAT IS YOUR GOOD NAME? ☆

This is another Indian English phrase. While Juliet in Shakespeare's *Romeo and Juliet* may have said, 'What's in a name? A rose by any other name would smell as sweet', to suggest that the names of things do not affect what they really are, the words 'good name' to ask someone what they are called is specific and particular to Indian English. The phrase is most likely a direct translation from the question in Hindi: '*Aapka shubh naam kyan hein?*' *Shubh* translated from Hindi is an adjective that accords the name an auspicious or good meaning.

⭐ MUGGING UP ⭐

When I was growing up in India, we often had to 'mug up' to do well at school. Mugging up usually meant memorizing and regurgitating our text in exams. Of course, anywhere else in the world, if you are caught mugging it usually means you are caught stealing, and the reward is a jail sentence, not high marks on a test! And if you were mugged, most likely you were stopped by a thief and had to give away your phone and wallet!

⭐ CONVENT-EDUCATED ⭐

Well, I know that my parents told their friends that their daughters were 'convent-educated'. But this did not mean that we studied in a nunnery. It is true that our school was run by the Catholic diocese and we did have many teachers in the school who were nuns. But this term, used mostly in India, referred to an all-girls school in which the medium of instruction was English. The term is now used more broadly to refer to any educational institution run by nuns.

⭐ SITTING ON MY HEAD ⭐

This hilarious phrase sounds like someone has actually climbed up your shoulders and is seated on the top of your head. 'Get down. You are heavy,' is what I feel like saying. But the words are a direct translation from the Hindi colloquial statement that goes *'mere sir pe baitha hai'*—and means that the person is put under stress by someone in a position of authority, perhaps a teacher or a parent. The phrase is quite similar to *'mera dimag kha raha hai'*, which literally translates to eating my brains!

⭐ PREPONE ⭐

If you are unable to do something at the appointed time, you postpone the task or the meeting. But in India if you want to reschedule the meeting to an earlier time, that's 'preponing' it. Quite ingenious, if you ask me. And 'pre' is the literal antonym for 'post', so it makes perfect sense.

⭐ OUT OF STATION ⭐

This phrase has little to do with railways. It's used regularly in India to suggest that someone is out of town. So, 'I was out of station' is often an excuse given for not being at work, school or even at that important meeting you forgot to prepone or postpone.

*But **words** are things, and a small drop of ink,*
Falling like dew, upon a thought,
produces that which makes thousands,
perhaps millions, think.

—George Gordon, Lord Byron, English Romantic poet

What You Can Do with Your Words

SESTUDES

A sestude is a free-form piece (somewhat poetic in nature) that has exactly 62 words. Like 100-word stories, creating sestudes is a reflective writing exercise that requires adhering to a precise word length. Writers can use their powers of observation and imagination to describe a person, place or thing. This exercise encourages one to select words carefully and judiciously. I'm sharing a few sestudes on the theme of travel because I love to visit new places. Read these as examples and write a sestude on some other subject/topic of your choice.

✫ SESTUDES ON TRAVEL ✫

1. Tanzania is the land of Mount Meru and shy Kilimanjaro always behind cloud cover. I learned that there are 120 proud tribes in the bush, and the Masai remain the tallest. Benches made from jacaranda, cypress, mahogany invite you to sit and rest in style as you explore. 'Jambo!' say the East Africans as they welcome you. Tanzania called Hemingway as well.

2. We drove from the airport to the Las Vegas strip, where our resort hid behind the glitter and glass of the casinos. It had been a decade since we visited Sin City's gambling scene. 60 million years ago, tectonic plates shifted on the floor of the ocean and pushed up rocks and eroded sand to lay the floor for this shining place.

3. Red Rock Canyon National Park can be found in Nevada's Mojave Desert. We walked the 3 km Moenkopi Trail and saw the expanse of seashells that were once on the bottom of an ocean floor and had calcified over thousands of years into limestone. The red rock sandstone peaks and calico hills soared behind us. It was such a picture-perfect postcard view.

4. Valley of Fire State Park has unusual 'beehive' formations of red sandstone. We climbed stairs attached to ancient rock walls to see 4000-year-old petroglyphs. There was once a thriving civilization here. The park was spectacular—vast, colourful and rugged. This was a place that had withstood the test of erosion and time from when the dinosaurs roamed it a million years ago.

5. In four weeks of travel through India we rediscovered that the monsoons in Kerala have an uncommon beauty and fragrance, that Chennai is cooler in mid-June than in mid-December, that sanitation on city streets is still a problem throughout the country and also that smart innovators in Bengaluru are inking carbon out of foul air and turning exhaust fumes into useful ink.

6. I learned that city editions of national newspapers in India look beyond local news. Today's paper featured an inspiring story of a Swiss entrepreneur set to bring cheaper X-rays to Africa, a laudable piece about food recycling in Ireland, another about the Indian moringa tree fighting climate change in Tunisia and even about a Japanese company turning old, discarded clothes into ethanol!

7. Guatemala is known as 'Land of Volcanoes' because there are 37 volcanoes in the country and 6 active volcanoes that make up the 'ring of fire'. A guide told us that Volcon Pacaya would be easy and accessible. But it was not. In fact, it was a steep hike and brutal on the knees as the ascent is littered with hard stones.

8. Pat Tillman Memorial Bridge connects Nevada and Arizona. It is a long arch bridge over the Colorado river and has a 6-foot-wide pedestrian sidewalk that runs its entire length. We didn't walk across the bridge, but we took photos. The bridge is 890 feet high and is the second-highest bridge in America. Looking over at Hoover Dam from the bridge is amazing.

WRITE YOUR OWN SESTUDE

*The best **word** shakers were the ones who understood the true power of **words**. They were the ones who could climb the highest.*

—Markus Zusak, Australian writer

How Many Sounds Can a C Make?

How many sounds can a C make?

I bet you'd like to know.

It's usually hard like a /k/ sound,

Unless *e, i, y* follows like so—

Thus *cease, cider, cyber* and *cedar*,

Sound like /s/ when C's the letter.

But with an *a, o* or *u* for a hard sound,

We hear /kuh/ like in *capital, contain* and *capture*.

The silent C is quite unusual,

When paired with the letter S.

It makes no sound as when not heard in *scissor*,

But *school*, and *scandal*—just take a guess!

The quiet C has a /ʃ/ sound,

It's what we hear in *precious* and *social*.

And *ocean* stays within the rule,

But *ocelot* remains quite special!

And C with an h has its own rules,

We hear both /tʃ/ and /kuh/ sometimes.

When ch starts the word, it sounds soft, like 'change',

But when in the middle, a hard 'echo' it chimes.

Well, it wouldn't be English without a few exceptions,

And it wouldn't be English without these words

And now that C sounds have been illustrated,

You've learned the right rules and the absurd!

Words, *like nature, half reveal and half conceal the soul within.*

—Alfred, Lord Tennyson, English poet

The Sound of Silence

What do you (k)now about silent letters?

You see them in words, plain as day.

In some cases, to speak them is tricky,

But there are a few rules that help what to say.

Before n, k is silent as in *knowledge*,

And *knife, knitting* and *kneel*.

And gh is quiet after ou,

Thought, through and *dough* is the deal.

We don't hear the b in *subtle*,

We don't hear the l in *talk*.

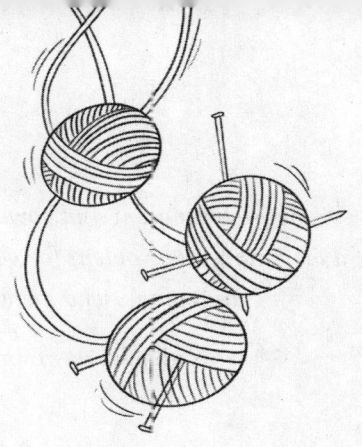

And where's the t in *whistle*?

Like the l it went for a *walk*!

The w in *written* is silent,

Wrestle and *wrong* are more clues.

The sound of /w/ is removed by /r/,

And we know this as one of the rules.

The /p/ sound in *psychology* is missing,

Pseudo and *Psalm's* p is quiet too.

When s follows p at the start of a word,

You now know what to say and do.

In *rendezvous* the z is silent,

It's a French word as you can tell.

So the order of letters affects sound,

The origin of the word does as well.

Words—so innocent and powerless as they are, as standing in a dictionary, how potent for good and evil they become, in the hands of one who knows how to combine them!

—Nathaniel Hawthorne, American novelist

Vocabulary—Zany Words from A to Z
Learn a new word every day

Here are a few zany words from me. Can you come up with another list from A to Z?

Allocution: a formal speech that gives advice or warning. Don't confuse the word with elocution, which is the skill of expressive speech.

Battologize: to annoy someone by repeating the same thing over and over again. And again. And again.

Cachinnate: to laugh loudly and inappropriately

Daedalist: an aviator or a pilot. Who knew?

Eirenism: a peaceful state of mind. This is a word we should all learn swiftly.

Fartlek: what athletes do when they alternate between sprinting and jogging

Grumbletonian: A habitual complainer

Hellion: a mischievous troublemaker

Iatrophobia: fear of going to a doctor

Jackanapes: a mischievous child

Kibitzer: a backseat driver

Logodaedalist: one skilled in using or coining words

Misophonia: an intolerance of certain sounds, such as chewing, slurping, etc.

Remember the sound of chalk on the blackboard?

Noob: perhaps you knew this one. A noob is someone who is inexperienced. It's most often used when your sibling isn't playing that video game too well.

Octothorpe: I had thought the symbol # was called a hashtag. But it's actually an octothorpe.

Pronk: you know that leap you do in the air when you have an arched back and stiff legs, well, that's a pronk!

Quin: short for quintuplet

Ratoon: not an animal; a tiny shoot growing from the root of a plant

Stumblebum: a clumsy person

Talpa: a mole or similar mark on the body

Ughten: the part of the night immediately before daybreak

Verbomaniac: yes, it is a person who has a craze for words.

Wamble-worn: when you are feeling nauseous, you look wamble-worn

Xenops: a small tropical bird found in the rainforests

Yaff: to bark like a snarling dog

Zebrinny: the offspring of a male horse and a female zebra

Words can be like X-rays if you use them properly—they'll go through anything. You read and you're pierced.

—Aldous Huxley, English writer and philosopher

Parts of Speech

There are eight parts of speech that build words,

Let's list them, discover and use.

The NOUN names *you*, *there* and *that*,

People, places and things are the cues.

Common nouns are words ordinary,

Proper nouns with capitals do rule.

Even a skilled public speaker,

On parts of speech will need to be schooled.

PRONOUNS may seem a tough topic,

But they can be just simply told.

A pronoun is used in place of a noun,
Personal, or possessive and bold.
You, it, we, us and they,
She, her, he, him, I, me.
When possessive: it's *my, your* and *its,*
His, her, our, their, whose—just see.
We know that a VERB expresses action,
Subject and verb form a sentence.
The verb must agree with the subject,
Heed singular and plural or there's vengeance!
An ADJECTIVE adds colour and description,
It details the pronoun or noun.
Helps answer *which one? What kind? And how many?*
Red pants, *soft* apple and buildings *brown.*
ADVERBS are similar to adjectives,
But modified verbs are the words we see.
They usually answer some questions,
Of *when, where, how, why* and to *what degree.*
Speak *slowly,* know *well,* run *swiftly,*
Add information to what we know.
Adverbs usually end with an 'ly',
Sometimes rules get broken; words come and go.
PREPOSITIONS are words or phrases,

Used before noun and pronoun with ease.

Show place, time, direction, like *out of, in, to* and *for*,

As: a mouse hid *under* the table for cheese.

Joining words, clauses and phrases,

CONJUNCTIONS link sections that are equal.

Using *for, nor, but, so, to* and others,

Coupling phrases to build sentence and sequel.

Shout out with INTERJECTIONS, express emotion,

Use exclamations liberally too.

Yay, wow, uh oh, oops and yikes!

Blah, yuck and alas, when you are blue.

There are eight parts of speech in sentence structure,

Let's list them, discover and use.

It may be hard to remember all details,

Fear not, this poem has ignited the fuse!

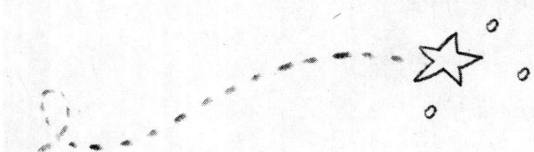

*My task, which I am trying to achieve is, by the power of the written **word**, to make you hear, to make you feel, it is, before all, to make you see.*

—Joseph Conrad, Polish-British writer

Epilogue

Speaking, writing and reading are essential to our everyday life. And WORDS help us do all three, as they are the tools for expression, communication and even connection. Through the words we use, whether consciously or unconsciously, we are revealing ourselves to others but also to ourselves. Language helps us understand ourselves.

I leave you with a list of thoughts about WORDS spoken by poets, philosophers and other wise people. I also end this book with a short essay I wrote about WORDS that was selected for a radio broadcast as part of a series called *Perspective* in San Francisco, California, in 2009.

*Better than a thousand hollow **words** is one word that brings peace.*

—Gautama Buddha, religious teacher

*Raise your **words**, not your voice. It is rain that grows flowers, not thunder.*

—Rumi, 13th century Persian poet

*Silence is better than unmeaning **words**.*

—Pythagoras, Greek philosopher

*Kind **words** can be short and easy to speak, but their echoes are truly endless.*

—Mother Teresa, Indian-Albanian catholic nun

***Words** have a magical power. They can either bring the greatest happiness or the deepest despair.*

—Sigmund Freud, Austrian neurologist and founder of psychoanalysis

***Words** are but pictures of our thoughts.*

—John Dryden, 17th century English poet

*It is better in prayer to have a heart without **words**
than **words** without a heart.*

—Mohandas Karamchand Gandhi, Indian lawyer,
freedom fighter and social activist

***Words** mean more than what is set down on paper. It takes the
human voice to infuse them with deeper meaning.*

—Maya Angelou, American poet and civil rights activist

*Language creates reality. **Words** have power.
Speak always to create joy.*

—Deepak Chopra, Indian-American author and practitioner of
alternate medicine

***Words** can inspire. And words can destroy. Choose yours well.*

—Robin Sharma, Canadian writer

***Words** empty as the wind are best left unsaid.*

—Homer, Greek author of the *Iliad* and the *Odyssey*

*All big changes of the world come from **words**.*

—Marjane Satrapi, French-Iranian graphic novelist

On Words

I have loved words ever since I was a little girl. As a child, I read poems aloud and listened to words roll off my tongue. 'Over the cobbles he clattered and clashed,' I recited. Words like **rattle** and *sizzle* made me **buzz** with excitement.

It all started with elocution classes at a Calcutta convent. We were taught the story of Demosthenes, the Greek orator, who overcame his stammer by speaking with pebbles in his mouth. Demosthenes learned to enunciate his words and control his speech. And we, too, with our practiced '**Ts**' and perfect '**Os**', would soon be master speechmakers.

'Ann met an ant and an ant met Ann,' I sounded each /t/ deliberately. 'Hell**o** said the ant. Hell**o** said Ann.' The /o/ was lengthened, as were the other vowels.

Then it was tongue twisters. 'Betty Botter bought a bit of butter. But the butter Betty Botter bought was bitter…' Once I had mastered that ditty, I was hooked. Who wouldn't want to play with words? It was so much fun.

Today, I know words are more than fun. Powerful public speaking is the signature of everyone from a voiceover artist to a politician. Regardless of who we are, there's a good chance that someday we will be asked to make a speech. Whether it's a toast at a graduation or a roast at a wedding, it is useful to be prepared for that public presentation.

Like Demosthenes, we all have pebbles to overcome—challenges that force us to translate thoughts in ways we never thought possible. For fifteen years, I worked in non-profit development, using my voice to give voice to others. And the lessons I learned as a little girl continued to serve me: when you love language—its sounds and idiosyncrasies—you take special care to use words well. Today, my hope is that when words emerge from my mouth, you, too, will hear them come alive.

With a perspective—this is Shobha Tharoor Srinivasan

Psst! You can use this space to list new words that you discover, solve word puzzles, practise writing exercises or play word games. Feel free to explore the English language as you like!

About the author

Shobha Tharoor Srinivasan is the author of a dozen books of fiction and nonfiction and an award-winning voice-over artist who received the Silver Lotus Award for Best Narration at the 68th National Film Awards, India (2022). Her distinctive, mellifluous voice has brought life to documentaries, educational programs, journalistic initiatives and audiobooks—including her own stories. Shobha's writing has been widely anthologized and selected for school curricula by leading educational publishers in India. A frequent speaker at literary festivals and panel discussions, she has been featured on radio and television, profiled in magazines and had one of her stories performed by Silicon Valley Shakespeare in California. Prior to her literary and voice work, Shobha spent two decades as a nonprofit development professional, advocating for and fundraising on behalf of people with disabilities.

About the illustrator

A visual artist and a design graduate from NIFT, Delhi, **Isha Nagar** creates fantasy-like illustrations and artworks for children. Until now, she has worked on books like *Fishbowl, We Care, The Ghost of Malabar, V for Vaccine* and *What Is a Tail Good For*, among others. In her free time, she is found swimming in the gigantic waves of watercolours, with little pauses to sniff new books. She has worked with publishers like HarperCollins India, Penguin Random House, Duckbill books and Room to Read to name a few. You can view her work at www.ishanagar.com.

HarperCollins *Publishers* India

At HarperCollins India, we believe in telling the best stories and finding the widest readership for our books in every format possible. We started publishing in 1992; a great deal has changed since then, but what has remained constant is the passion with which our authors write their books, the love with which readers receive them, and the sheer joy and excitement that we as publishers feel in being a part of the publishing process.

Over the years, we've had the pleasure of publishing some of the finest writing from the subcontinent and around the world, including several award-winning titles and some of the biggest bestsellers in India's publishing history. But nothing has meant more to us than the fact that millions of people have read the books we published, and that somewhere, a book of ours might have made a difference.

As we look to the future, we go back to that one word—a word which has been a driving force for us all these years.

Read.